THE ANDREW LLOYD WEBBER ANTHOLOGY

Exclusively Distributed by

7777 West Bluemound Road P.O. Box 13819 Milwaukee, WI 53213

ISBN No. 0.88188.960.1
PRODUCT No. HL 00359075

EXCLUSIVE DISTRIBUTORS IN U.K. & EIRE:
MUSIC SALES LIMITED
8/9 FRITH STREET, LONDON W1V 5TZ, ENGLAND

THIS EDITION © COPYRIGHT 1987 PUBLISHED BY THE REALLY USEFUL GROUP PLC
BY KIND PERMISSION OF THE COPYRIGHT OWNERS

BOOK DESIGNED BY
PEARCE MARCHBANK STUDIO

MUSIC EDITED AND ARRANGED BY
ROGER DAY

MUSIC ENGRAVING BY MUSIC PRINT LIMITED

JOSEPH AND THE AMAZING TECHNICOLOR® DREAMCOAT photograph reproduced
BY KIND PERMISSION OF DAVID LAND AND SUPERSTAR VENTURES LIMITED
GRANADA TELEVISION & GARY BOND
JESUS CHRIST SUPERSTAR photograph by LAURIE ASPREY
EVITA photograph by ZOË DOMINIC
CATS photograph by JOHN HAYNES
SONG AND DANCE photographs by NOBBY CLARK & MICHAEL LE POER TRENCH
REQUIEM photographs by CLIVE BARDA
STARLIGHT EXPRESS photograph by NOBBY CLARK
PHANTOM OF THE OPERA photograph by CLIVE BARDA

Andrew Lloyd Webber had his first piece of music published when he was nine. Now, not yet 40, he is the most successful British composer of musicals ever. He's written seven major hit musicals and he is the only composer to have had 3 shows running simultaneously in the West End and on Broadway. His name is in lights in most major capital cities around the world and more often than not his shows are the hottest ticket in town. The dazzle of his achievements can be blinding. This anthology shows its source: the tunes, the songs.

He has a talent rare in any area of music in any century: a gift for writing memorable melodies.

He had a fine grounding. Like many composers, Lloyd Webber grew up in a richly musical family. His father was a director of composition at the Royal College of Music – and subsequently Director at the London College of Music. His own compositions are now being re-recorded and released. "His father had this sense of melody and Andrew's inherited that, I'm sure", says his mother. She in her turn allowed her son the run of their flat to stage his earliest musical theatres and risked the wrath of neighbours as he played on one piano, her husband on another and Julian, his brother, attacked the cello.

He grew up in a home which seems to have been a hyperactive rehearsal room which was also a laboratory. When, in his mid teens, he met Tim Rice with whom he was to collaborate with such originality, he had already written 8 musicals.

Not only did he imbibe a classical musical education from his father, it was his father who brought the first rock'n'roll record into the house. One characteristic of Lloyd Webber's work has always been the ease and freshness with which he speaks different musical tongues: he is bi-lingual in classical and rock and can slip from one to the other with tremendous effect. He makes it fun. Wouldn't the 'Pie Jesu', he suggests, be marvellously sung by the Everly Brothers? "One can but dream".

A further element of course is his flair for and massive application to the details of musical theatre. It obsesses him: and the brilliant theatricality of the shows is proof of that relentless obsession.

Yet at the heart of the matter are the tunes. These fall into several groups of which the most striking are those which appeared at the time to be bold, even crazy and wholly unexpected. 'Jesus Christ Superstar' was a very high risk anthem when it was first suggested – blasphemous in those far off days. 'Don't Cry For Me Argentina' again, a song about a dictatrix in South America seemed as remote from the public taste as an interrogative pop song about the founder of the Christian religion: and as for 'Gus The Theatre Cat.' But again and again he stuck to his hunch, to his own musical genius and to the challenge of fine words which brought out the sinewy lyrical aspect of his talent.

He also has the ability to write music which is deeply moving 'I Don't Know How To Love Him', 'Memory', 'Pie Jesu', 'The Music Of The Night'. The melodies in themselves are touching and resonant. And where do you categorise 'Unexpected Song' – one of the best he has written in my opinion. He draws on many banks of musical experience.

This is a fair selection from 20 years' work. An indication of its richness is that 'Everything's All Right' (from 'Superstar') – a cunning and original piece – cannot find a place here. No doubt it will be included in the next anthology and no doubt there will be many more volumes to come. I have a feeling, to adapt Al Jolson, that "we ain't seen nothing yet".

Melvyn Bragg
18th September, 1987

JOSEPH AND THE AMAZING TECHNICOLOR DREAMCOAT

Close Every Door

Music by Andrew Lloyd Webber
Lyrics by Tim Rice

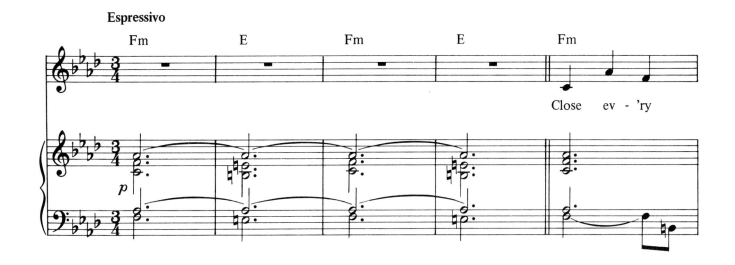

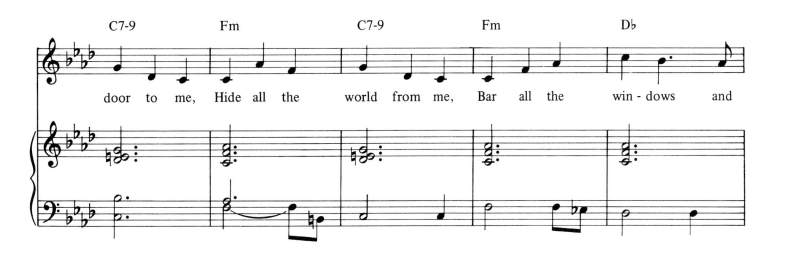

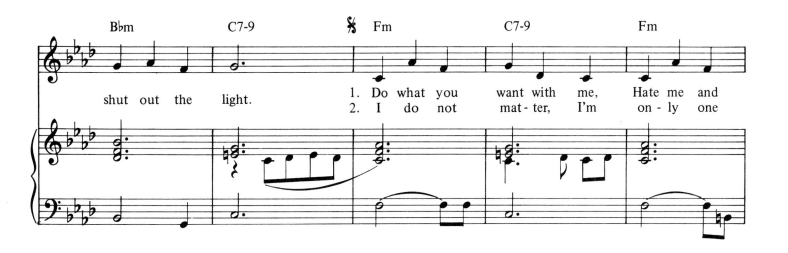

(Choir) La la la la la la, la la la la la la, La la la la la la, la la la la la la,

La la la la la la, la la la la la la, La la la la la la, la.

D.%. al Coda ⊕ **CODA**

Any Dream Will Do

Music by Andrew Lloyd Webber
Lyrics by Tim Rice

The world was wak - ing, a - ny dream will do.

A crash of drums, — a flash of light, — my gol - den coat flew

out of sight, — The col - ours fad - ed in - to dark - ness, I was left a -

lone. May I re - turn

JESUS CHRIST SUPERSTAR

JESUS CHRIST SUPERSTAR

MUSIC BY ANDREW LLOYD WEBBER
LYRICS BY TIM RICE

why'd you choose such a back-ward time and such a strange land? ____
could Ma - hom - et move a moun-tain or was that just P. R.? ____

If you'd come to - day you would have reached a whole na - tion,
Did you mean to die like that? Was that a mis - take ____ or

Is - rael in four B. C. had no mass com - mu - ni - ca - tion.)
did you know your mes - sy death would be a re - cord brea - ker?

(Don't you get me

wrong)   (don't you get me wrong now)   (don't you get me
Don't you get me wrong, ____   Don't you get me wrong ____

I Don't Know How To Love Him

Music by Andrew Lloyd Webber
Lyrics by Tim Rice

Slowly, tenderly and very expressively

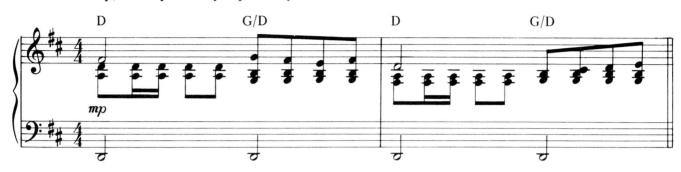

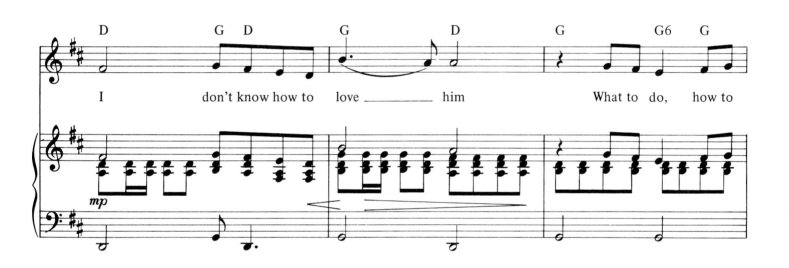

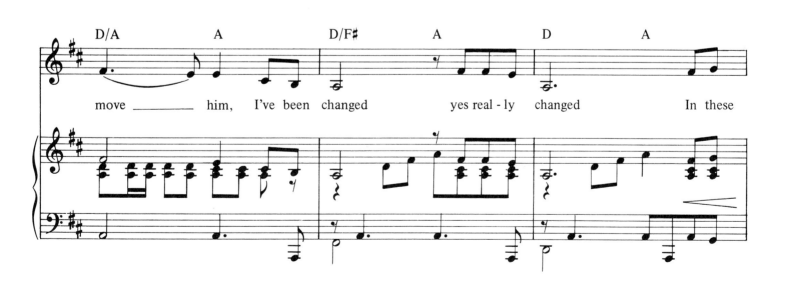

Herod's Song

Music by Andrew Lloyd Webber
Lyrics by Tim Rice

Moderato, ad lib.

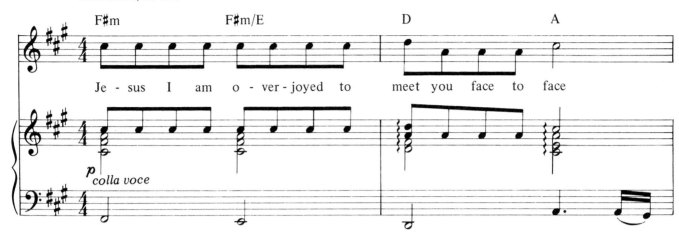

Moderato, ragtime style

said _____ So you are the Christ __ you're the great Je - sus Christ __
you are the Christ __ you're the great Je - sus Christ __

Prove to me that you're di - vine __ Change my wa - ter
Prove to me that you're no fool __ Walk a - cross my

in - to wine __ That's all you need do _____ and I'll know it's all true __
swim - ming pool __ If you do that for me _____ then I'll let you go free __

C'm - on King of the Jews. _____
C'm - on King of the

30

dy - ing to be shown that you are not just an-y man _____ So if

you are the Christ _____ yes the great Je - sus Christ _____

Feed my house-hold with this bread _____ you can do it on your head _____ Or has

some - thing gone wrong? _____ Why do you take so long? _____

Slowly – colla voce

C'm - on King of the Jews. Hey! Aren't you

accelerando, poco a poco

scared of me Christ? Mis - ter Won-der-ful Christ! You're a joke, you're not the Lord!

Moderato, ragtime style

You're noth - ing but a fraud — Take him a - way — he's got

noth - ing to say! — Get out you King of the

EVITA

Rainbow High

Music by Andrew Lloyd Webber
Lyrics by Tim Rice

I don't real-ly think I need the rea-sons why I

won't suc-ceed, I have done! Let's get this show on the road, let's make it

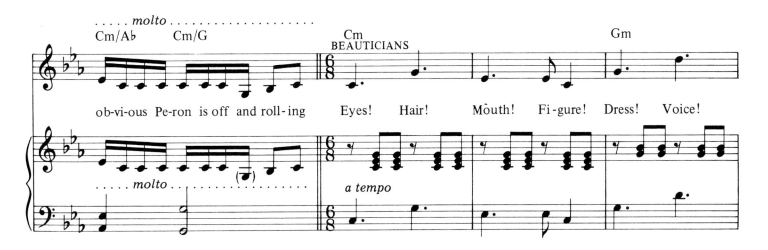

ob-vi-ous Pe-ron is off and roll-ing Eyes! Hair! Mouth! Fi-gure! Dress! Voice!

Don't Cry For Me Argentina

Music by Andrew Lloyd Webber
Lyrics by Tim Rice

try to ex-plain how I feel, That I still need your love af-ter all that I've done:

You won't be - lieve me All you will see is a girl you once knew Al -

though she's dressed up to the nines at six - es and sev - ens with you.

VERSE

2. I had to let it hap-pen, I had to change; Could-n't stay all my life down at heel: Look-ing

Horns

43

Another Suitcase In Another Hall

Music by Andrew Lloyd Webber
Lyrics by Tim Rice

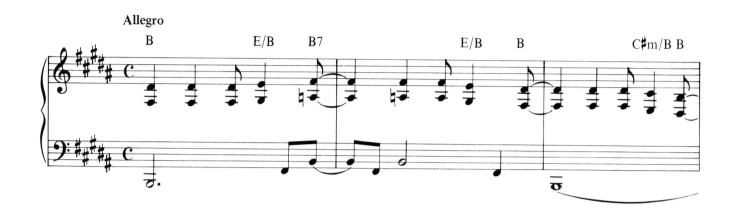

I don't ex- pect __ my
Time and time __ a -
Call in three __ months'

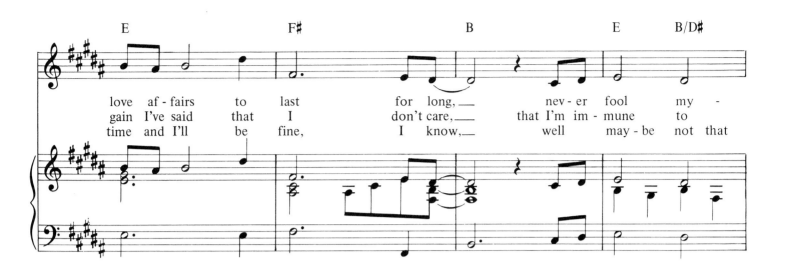

love af - fairs to last for long, __ nev - er fool my -
gain I've said that I don't care, __ that I'm im - mune to
time and I'll be fine, I know, __ well may - be not that

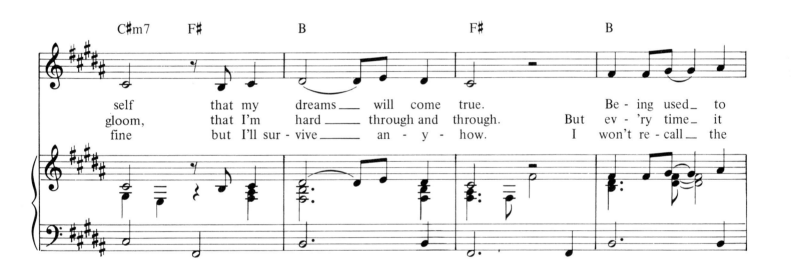

self that my dreams __ will come true. Be - ing used __ to
gloom, that I'm hard __ through and through. But ev - 'ry time __ it
fine but I'll sur - vive __ an - y - how. I won't re - call __ the

trou - ble, I __ an - ti - ci - pate __ it, but all the same I
mat - ters all __ my words de - sert __ me, so an - y - one can
names and pla - ces of this sad oc - ca - sion, but that's no con - so -

50

High Flying Adored

Music by Andrew Lloyd Webber
Lyrics by Tim Rice

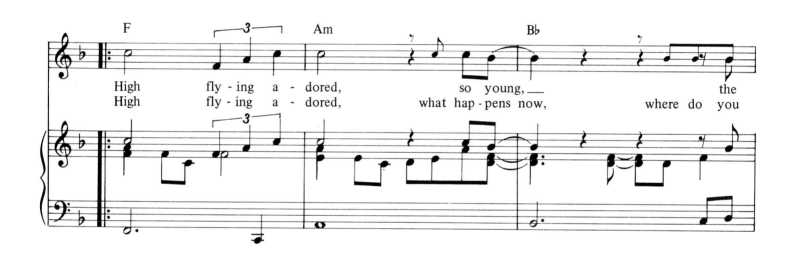

High fly-ing a-dored, so young,___ the
High fly-ing a-dored, what hap-pens now, where do you

in-stant queen.___ A___ rich beau-ti-ful thing of all the
go from here?___ For___ some-one on top of the world the

tal - ents, a cross be - tween __ a fan - ta - sy
view's not ex - act - ly clear, __ a shame __ you

of the bed
did it all

__ room and a saint.
__ at twen - ty six.

And you were just __ a back
There are no mys -

__ street girl, __
teries now, __

hust - ling and fight - ing,
no - thing can thrill __ you,

scratch - ing and bit - ing.
no one ful - fill __ you.

High fly - ing a - dored,
High fly - ing a - dored,

did you be - lieve
I hope you come

in your wild - est mo - ments
to terms with bore - dom.

CATS

MEMORY

Music by Andrew Lloyd Webber
Text by Trevor Nunn after T.S. Eliot

MR. MISTOFFELEES

Music by Andrew Lloyd Webber
Text by T.S. Eliot

look for a knife or a fork
in from the gar - den for hours,

And you think it is mere - ly mis-placed,
While he was a-sleep in the hall.

You have
And

C

seen it one mo - ment, and then it is gawn! But you'll find it next week _ ly - ing out on the lawn. _
not long a - go _ this phe-no-me-nal cat _ Pro - duced se - ven kit - tens right out of a hat! _

To Coda ⊕

C7

D.S. al Coda

And we all say:
And we all said:

f

⊕ **CODA** CHORUS

F   C/E   Gm7   C7

Oh! Well I ne-ver! Was _ there e - ver a cat so cle-ver as

F   F/A   B♭

1.   *Repeat ad lib.* | Last time

B♭/C   Dm

Ma - gi -cal Mis - ter Mis-tof - fel - ees!   fel - ees!

SOLO

Ladies and gentlemen, I give
you the marvellous, Magical
Mister Mistoffelees! Presto!

Gus The Theatre Cat

Music by Andrew Lloyd Webber
Text by T.S. Eliot

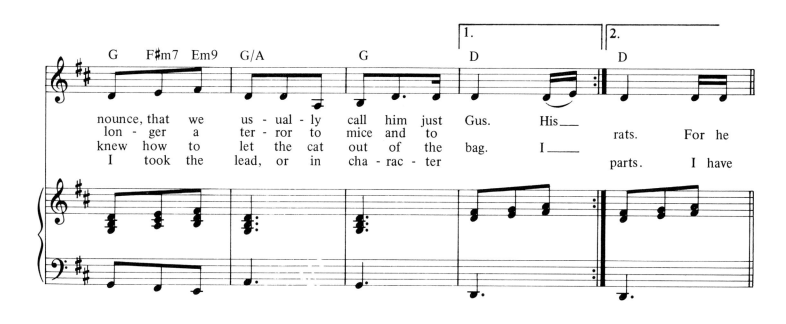

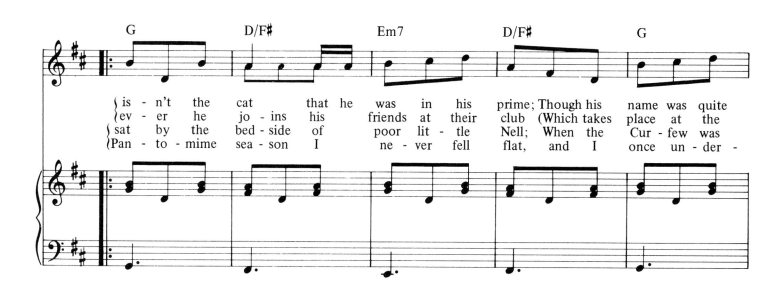

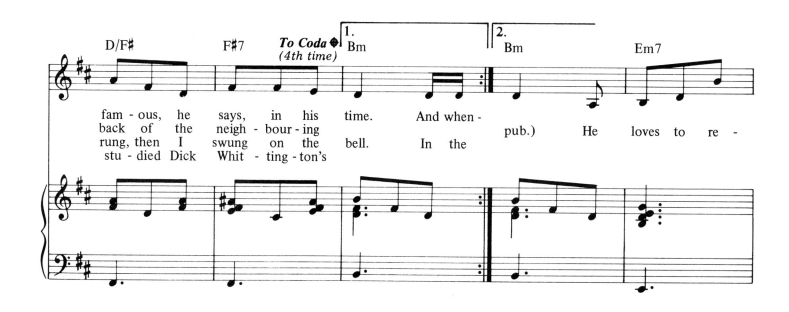

gale them, if some-one else pays, With an-ec-dotes drawn from his palm-i-est days.

For he once was a Star of the high-est de-gree: He has act-ed with
likes to re-late his suc-cess on the Halls, Where the Gal-le-ry

1.
Irv-ing, he's act-ed with Tree. And he
2.
once gave him sev-en cat-
calls. But his grand-est cre-a-tion, as

he loves to tell, Was Fire-frore-fid-dle, the Fiend of the Fell.

for-mance he once walked on pat, when some ac-tor sug-ges-ted the need for a cat. And I

say: Now, these kit-tens, they do not get trained As we did in the
nev-er get drilled in a re-gu-lar troupe, And they think they are

days when Vic-tor-i-a reigned. They
smart, just to jump through a hoop. And he says as he scratch-es him-

self with his claws: Well, the Thea-tre is cer-tain-ly not what it was. These

modern productions are all very well, but there's nothing to equal, from

what I hear tell. That moment of mystery When I made history As

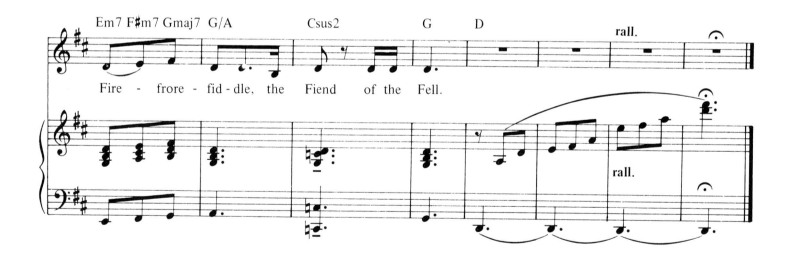

Firefrorefiddle, the Fiend of the Fell.

GUS *(Sung reprise)*

And I once crossed the stage on a telegraph wire,
To rescue a child when a house was on fire.
And I think that I still can much better than most,
Produce blood-curdling noises to bring on the Ghost.
I once played Growltiger, could do it again . . .

SONG AND DANCE

Tell Me On A Sunday

Music by Andrew Lloyd Webber
Lyrics by Don Black

Unexpected Song

Music by Andrew Lloyd Webber
Lyrics by Don Black

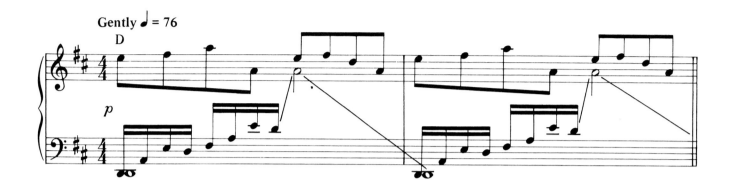

I
I have nev - er felt like this, for once I'm lost for
don't know what's go - ing on can't work it out at

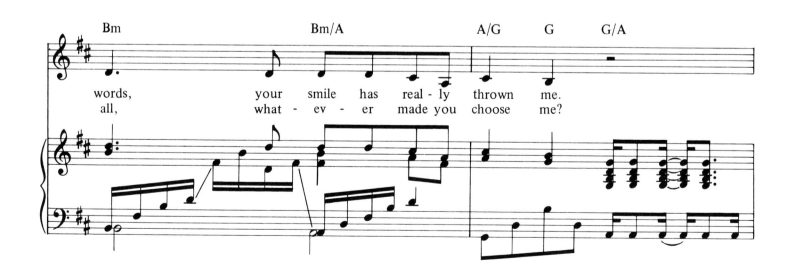

words, your smile has real - ly thrown me.
all, what - ev - er made you choose me?

Take That Look Off Your Face

Music by Andrew Lloyd Webber
Lyrics by Don Black

see through your smile,___ you would love to be right,___ I bet

you did-n't sleep good last night___ could-n't wait to bring

all of that bad__ news to my door, well I've got news for you__

I knew be-fore._____ (Take that

Take That Look Off Your Face (*REPRISE*)

Music by Andrew Lloyd Webber
Lyrics by Don Black

The Last Man In My Life

Music by Andrew Lloyd Webber
Lyrics by Don Black

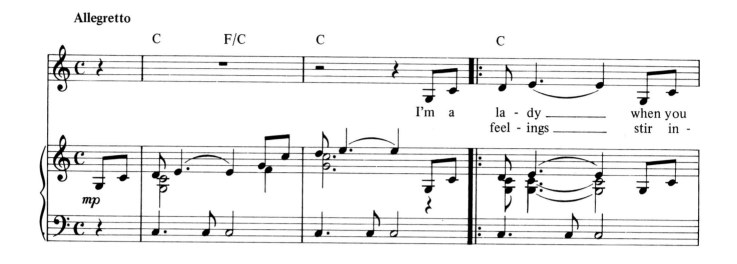

I'm a la - dy _____ when you
feel - ings _____ stir in -

kiss me, _____ I'm a child when you are leav - ing, _____ I'm a
side me, _____ used to think nights were for sleep - ing, _____ be - ing

wo - man _____ ev - 'ry time our bo - dies meet _____ com -
wan - ted _____ is a thrill I nev - er knew _____ till

REQUIEM

Pie Jesu

Music by Andrew Lloyd Webber

re-qui-em.

SOLO BOY *mp*

Pi - e Je - su, ___ pi - e Je - su, ___ pi - e

Ab

Bbm/Ab

Eb7/Ab

Ab

Qui tol - lis pec - ca - ta mun-di,

Je - su, ___ pi - e Je - su, Qui tol - lis pec - ca - ta mun-di,

SOPRANO

p

ALTO

Hm ___

TENOR

BASS

p

Bbm7/Db

Eb7

Db

Eb

Do - na e - is re - qui - em____ do - na e - is re - qui - em. ____

Do - na e - is re - qui - em, ___ do - na e - is re - qui - em. ____

Hm

Ab   Fm   Bbm7   Eb7   Ab   Abmaj7

mf

Ag - nus De - i, ____ Ag - nus

Ag - nus De - i, ___ Ag - nus

Ag - nus De - i, ___ Ag - nus

Ab6   Ab   Dbmaj7   Db/Eb Cm/Eb Bbm7/Ab

101

STARLIGHT EXPRESS

There's Me

Music by Andrew Lloyd Webber
Lyrics by Richard Stilgoe

Moderately

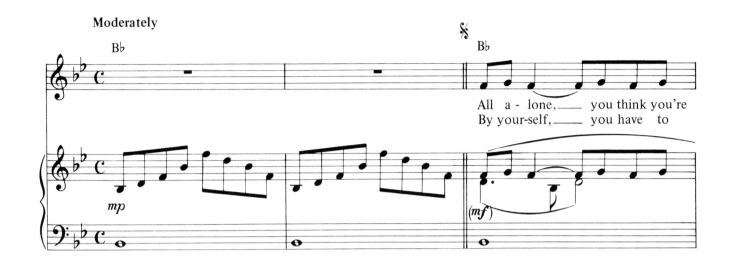

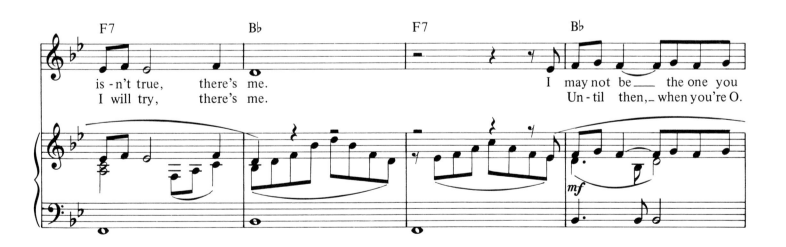

Starlight Express

Music by Andrew Lloyd Webber
Lyrics by Richard Stilgoe

Moderately

When your good - nights have been said __ and you are
take me a - way __ but bring me

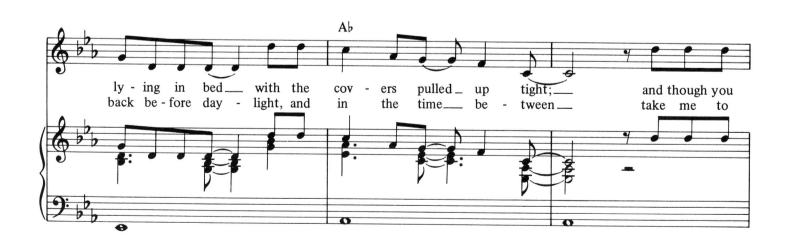

ly - ing in bed __ with the cov - ers pulled __ up tight; __ and though you
back be - fore day - light, and in the time __ be - tween __ take me to

ONLY YOU

Music by Andrew Lloyd Webber
Lyrics by Richard Stilgoe

113

Make Up My Heart

Music by Andrew Lloyd Webber
Lyrics by Richard Stilgoe

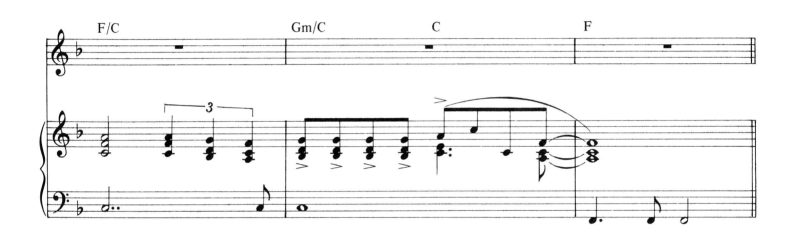

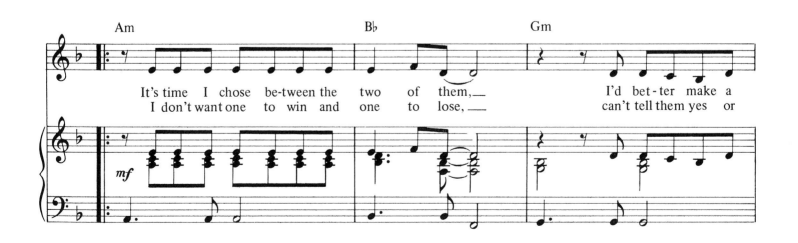

It's time I chose be-tween the two of them,___ I'd bet-ter make a
I don't want one to win and one to lose, ___ can't tell them yes or

117

PHANTOM OF THE OPERA

All I Ask Of You

Music by Andrew Lloyd Webber
Lyrics by Charles Hart
Additional lyrics by Richard Stilgoe

here, with you, be-side you, to guard you and to guide you.

CHRISTINE

All I ask is ev-ery wak-ing mo-ment, turn my head with talk of

sum-mer-time.___ Say you need me with you now and al-ways;

pro-mise me that all you say is true, that's all I ask of

122

124

Music Of The Night

Music by Andrew Lloyd Webber
Lyrics by Charles Hart
Additional lyrics by Richard Stilgoe

Andante

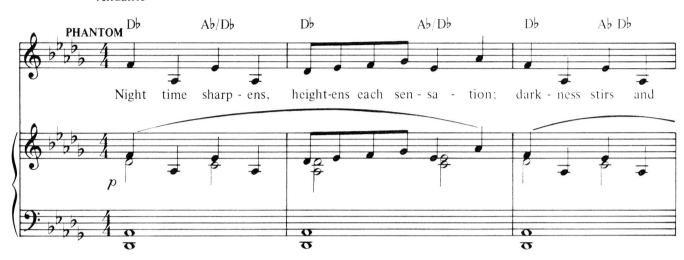

Night time sharp-ens, height-ens each sen-sa - tion: dark-ness stirs and

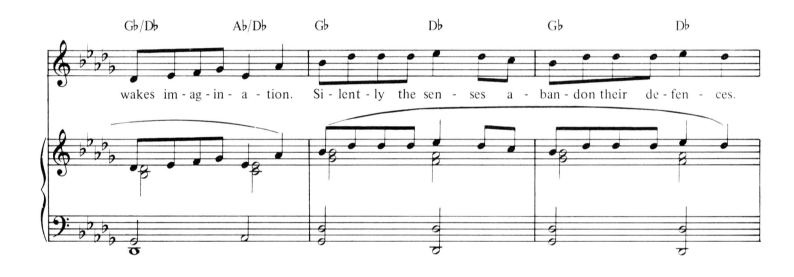

wakes im-ag-in-a - tion. Si - lent-ly the sen - ses a - ban-don their de-fen - ces.

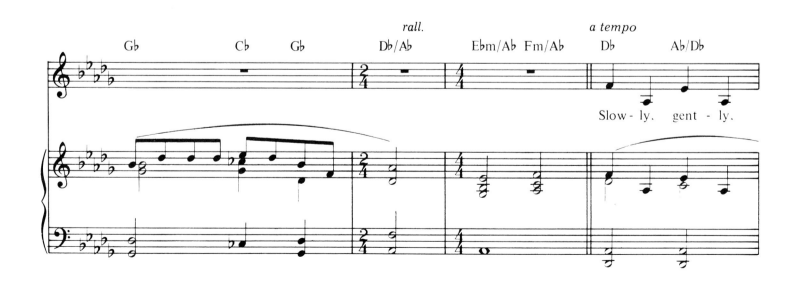

Slow - ly, gent - ly,

night un-furls its splen-dour; grasp it, sense it, trem-u-lous and ten-der.

Turn your face a-way from the gar-ish light of day, turn your thoughts a-way from cold, un-feel-ing

light and lis-ten to the mu-sic of the night. Close your eyes and sur-ren-der to your

dark-est dreams! Purge your thoughts of the life you knew be-fore! Close your

Wishing You Were Somehow Here Again

Music by Andrew Lloyd Webber
Lyrics by Charles Hart
Additional lyrics by Richard Stilgoe

You were once my one com-pan-ion,

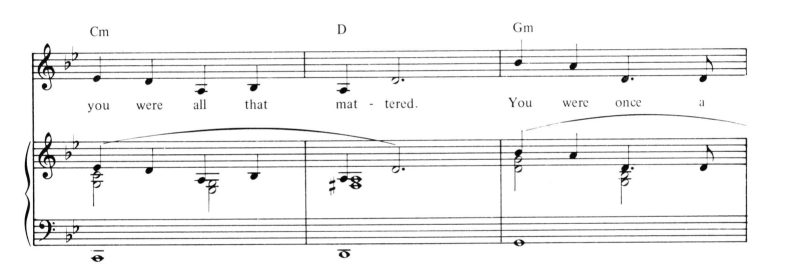

you were all that mat-tered. You were once a

friend and fa-ther, then my world was shat-tered.

The Phantom Of The Opera

Music by Andrew Lloyd Webber
Lyrics by Charles Hart
Additional lyrics by Richard Stilgoe & Mike Batt

Allegro – vivace

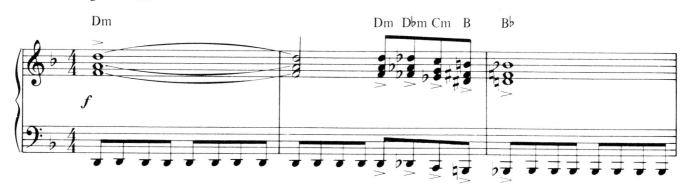

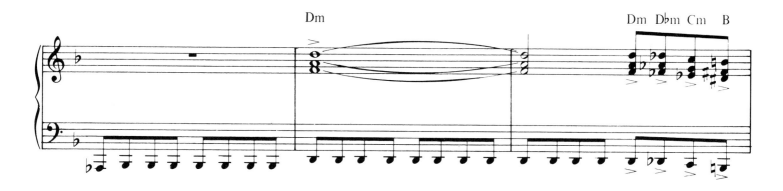

In sleep he sang to me, _____ in dreams he came,

that voice which calls to me _____ and speaks my name.

And do I dream a-gain? _____ for now I find _____

the phan - tom of the op-er-a is there _____

in - side my mind. _____

139

PHANTOM & CHRISTINE

Your spi - rit and my voice ____ in one com-
My spi - rit and your voice ____ in one com-

bined; ____ the phan - tom of the op-er-a is
bined; ____ the phan - tom of the op-er-a is

VOICES

He's *there,* *the* *phan -* *tom of* *the*
there in - side my mind.
there in - side your mind.

op - era. ____ *Be -* *ware* *the* *phan -* *tom of* *the*